T0197418

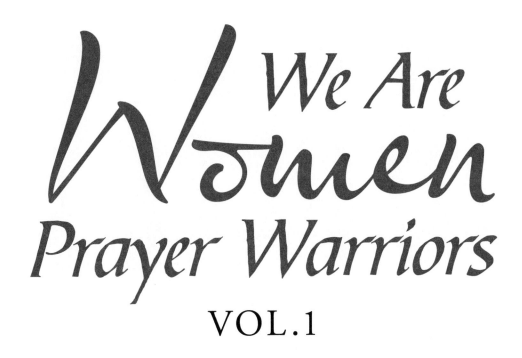

We Are Women Prayer Warriors

VOL.1

BRAVE SOULS

AUTHOR: *Elena Quevedo, MD Disciple of God*
CO-AUTHOR: *Stephanie St. Marie Disciple of God*

To order additional copies of this book, please contact:
Palibrio
1663 Liberty Drive
Suite 200
Bloomington, IN 47403
Toll Free from the U.S.A 877.407.5847
Toll Free from Mexico 01.800.288.2243
Toll Free from Spain 900.866.949
From other International locations +1.812.671.9757
Fax: 01.812.355.1576
orders@palibrio.com

Library of Congress Control Number: 2022951470
ISBN: 978-1-5065-4920-0 (sc)
ISBN: 978-1-5065-4921-7 (e)

Print information available on the last page

Rev date: 06/05/2023

HOLY BIBLE NVI
REYNA VALERA 60
LA BIBLIA VERSION
Rebecca Brown MD.:
PREPARE FOR WAR, Page
106 ,1987
TORA BIBLE
Clayton Ellen:THE COMPLETE FEMALE WARRIORS 2018

We Are Women Prayer Warriors

iv

Dedicated to

God because he is powerful, awesome, wonderful, merciful, and most of all LOVING

God is a giver, healer, our Savior

My beloved Sister friend, Maureen Palmer because she is a special disciple of God

Acknowledgements:

I wish to acknowledge Karla Osorio. She is a 19-year-old student studying communication and international affairs at the University of Michigan located in Ann Arbor, Michigan. In her free time, she enjoys writing. Her parents are Efrain Osorio and Adelina Sanchez Hernandez. They are incredibly supportive of Karla.

I wish to acknowledge Alberto Loyola. "I want to fulfill my responsibilities as a father and a husband."

"As a kid, I saw poverty in my family, and experienced how hard life is for a small boy. I watched my parents and siblings working hard working at diverse sources of income to put food on the table. Sometimes there wouldn't be anything to eat for 2 days. At an early age, I became a farmer, a fisherman, and a sales boy. I sold vegetables, metal items, empty bottles, coconuts, fruits, all kinds of sea food, anything that could be sold. Even newspapers, cartoons, chickens, eggs, and pigs."

"As a kid, I always wanted to be a good person, a responsible human being that cared for everything and all living things. Again, I promised myself that I would be a good husband and father to my kids one day ensuring that my kids would have a better future. And to teach them how to deal with the hardships in life."

Rich Keiper is also acknowledged here. He served in the Korean War. He likes to make people laugh. He believes in the Trinity. He worked in the automotive industry for 31 years. He started to write in the 90's. Using his imagination and his religion to write.

The last person I wish to acknowledge is Pastor Ryan Kolander who is my spiritual director. He is a wonderful spiritual leader and serves beyond what people ever expect a pastor to do.

1. "Yeshua" the real name of Jesus from the Torah Bible. "Heaven and earth will pass away, but my WORDS will not pass away," Mark 13: 31.
2. Rejoice always, pray continually, give thanks in all circumstances, for this is God's will for you and Christ Jesus," 1 Thessalonians 5: 16
3. Keep Yeshua at the core of everything.

Elena and Stephanie St. Marie

Why We are Writing this Book

Stephanie and I are writing this book because we love God, and we want you to know and love him as well. This book is for you, your families, and friends all over the world.

I am disabled and in a wheelchair from a spinal cord injury. I want to reach out to those who find themselves in a similar position.

Keep God in your heart and always on your mind throughout every waking minute of your day. Become a prayer Warrior because satan is desperate and he knows that Yeshua is coming soon. He is attacking those who are close to God.

Table of Contents

Introduction

I was born in Panama City, Central America in an apartment on March 18, 1951. My mother's name was Ruby Lina Barley who was a devoted Christian and raised us in a "Godly" fashion. She only went through the fourth grade but taught herself how to read perfectly. She read a book every month, was sweet, charming, loving, and much more. She died in 1999.

My father's name was Larin Perry, an alcoholic that abused me sexually, and my mother physically, emotionally, and more. He also abused my three brothers (Larin Perry, Floyd Johnson, and Alberto Johnson).

This book is about our love for Yeshua. It contains interviews, testimonials about miracles, confessions, where we came from, why we are here, and where we are headed.

You will learn how to deal with satanic forces.

BUT MOST OF ALL ITS ABOUT THE POWER OF PRAYER COMING FROM WOMEN PRAYER WARRIORS BRAVE SOULS.

God is everything to us. He is the reason for our lives. Because of Him, we get up every day, we wake up with Him, and go to sleep with Him on our minds every day. He gives us peace, love, and more. We try to live Godly lives, although it's difficult sometimes. We want eternal life. We adore God, He has done so much for us.

My Commitment to God

I, Elena Quevedo, make this commitment to God, to myself, to my family, and to my friends… that I will make every effort to always live according to the commandments of God.

Elena Quevedo October 18, 2022

I have been a disciple and a Prayer Warrior for the past 15 years and I have had multiple battles with satanic forces.

But with the help of God, I have always been able to call on Yeshua to help cast the evil away.

We are undergoing continuous satanic attack.

CHAPTER 1 –

Definition of a Prayer Warrior

Prayer Warriors is a term used by many Evangelical and other Christians referring to anyone who is committed to praying for others to save souls and to defend God's commandments.

Prayer Warriors battle against demonic forces. They can pray for individuals as well as for nations and peoples anywhere.

Prayer Warriors mentioned in the Bible are described as advocates who feel themselves called to the Ministry of Reconciliation, the most important relationship between man and God.

The heart of a Prayer Warrior is fashioned after God's own love. It is a selfless love that looks beyond one's self and truly seeks God's will.

Characteristics of a Prayer Warrior include being worshipful, always seeking to glorify the Lord, and they are God-centered, focusing on His Love and Mercy.

They are intuitive and empathic, able to meet and accept people where they are.

Prayer Warriors are always prepared to take on the Spiritual battles encountered daily.

CHAPTER 2 –

Spiritual Warfare

Spiritual Warfare requires Wisdom "one who aspires to enlightenment or a heroic being."

There are four key elements to prayer

1. Adoration
2. Confession
3. Thanksgiving
4. Supplication

The power of prayer depends on one's relationship with God. One must pray with faith that God is listening and answers prayers. This dynamic relationship is powerful and fulfilling. We pray to God in the name of Yeshua. For spiritual growth we follow in His footsteps as He taught us

1. Pray daily
2. Pray fervently
3. Pray without ceasing
4. Pray with expectation

5. Pray and act when God gives guidance
6. Pray through your fear
7. Pray as a disciple

What does a Warrior Spirit mean? It means using the Creator-given talent and ability to be an asset to family, community, coworkers, and friends. A Warrior Spirit extends this to God's entire world.

Discover your Warrior Spirit. You can learn to lead a more rewarding life.

What is YOUR definition of a Warrior Spirit?

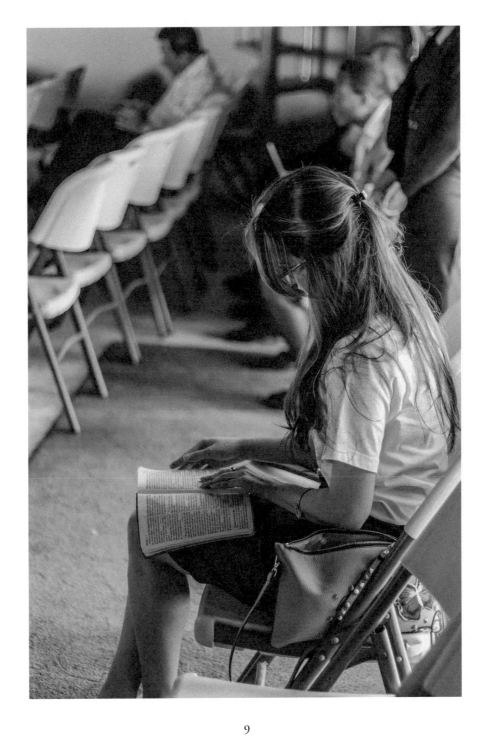

CHAPTER 3 –

The Holy Bible's Description of Women Prayer Warriors

Judges 4:4 "…Deborah the Prophetess, the wife of Lappidoth, a leader of Israel at that time"

Judges 4:5 "She held court under the palm of Deborah between Ramah and Bethel in the hill country. Ephraim and the Israelites came to her to have their disputed decided"

Ephesians 6:10 "Finally be strong in the Lord and His mighty power. Put on the full armor of God so that you can take your stand against the devil's schemes."

Esther 7:3-4 "Then Esther the Queen, answered and said, if I have found favor in thy sight, and if it please the King, let my life be given at my petition and my people at my request…We are a people to be sold, to be sane, and to perish"

Romans 5:3-5 "…we rejoice in our suffering knowing that suffering produces endurance. And endurance produces character, and character produces hope. And hope does not put us to shame because God's love has been poured into our hearts through the Holy Spirit who has been given to us.

Esther 4:14 "For if you remain silent at this time, relief and deliverance for the Jews will arise from another place. But you and your father's family will perish and who knows but that you have come to royal position for such time as this."

Matthew 28:20 "…teach them everything I have commanded you and surely I am with you always to the very end of the age"

Song of Songs 4:7 "You are altogether beautiful my darling, there is no flaw in you.

Isaiah 43:2 "When you pass through the waters, I will be with you and when you pass through the rivers, they will not sweep over you. When you walk through the fire, you will not be burned. The flames will not set you ablaze."

Proverbs 21:21 "Whoever pursues righteousness and love finds life, prosperity, and honor."

Proverbs 17:1 "Better is a dry morsal with quiet than a house full feasting with strife."

CHAPTER 4

Women Warriors According to the Holy Bible

There are few examples of Women Warriors in the Bible. Recognized are Deborah, Esther, Ruth, Jaels, Judith, and the unnamed women of Thebez.

Deborah was the only female judge of Israel; she led the Israeli army into war against the Canaanites. Deborah led he Canaanite General into her tent and killed him with a tent peg through the head.

Deborah became a singular Biblical figure, a female military leader, and a rare Biblical character.

She trusted God completely. God told Deborah to command Barak, one of the Generals of the Lord's army, to go into battle against Sisera, the commander of the enemy army. God promised Deborah that he would deliver Sisera into Barak's hands. Deborah was strong and brave, also a prophetess. She was a hybrid of military commander and governor.

Esther was a young Jewish woman living in the Persian region who found favor with the King of Persia, became Queen, and risked her life saving the Jewish people from destruction.

One of the characteristics of Esther in the Bible was her willingness to yield to the wishes of others. She was very obedient. The story of Esther written in the Bible may sound like a fairy tale, but it was more about God moving among his people to secure Israel's future.

The Bible contains the story of a woman Ruth, that after being widowed by her husband, remains with her mother-in-law. Her story is celebrated during the Jewish festival of Shavot, the 50 days following Passover.

Her stories in the book of Ruth, which encourages us to view our day to day lives as part of God's greater plan.

This book taught the Israelites how obedience could bring blessings to their lives.

Jaels is a case of Biblical antiquities making her character seductive in nature. She shows a spirit of romance for God, praying to God for guidance when Sisera was in her tent. She fulfilled religious obligations, a deeply religious woman.

Judith's story comes after Jaels. Judith is found in a book written in a Jewish holy text. The Book of Judith was included in the Christian Old Testament and is still considered authoritative for Roman Catholics and Eastern Orthodox Catholics today. She killed Holafernes, the general of Assyrians with his own sword, saving Israel. Judith died at the age of 105.

The Unknown woman of Thebez appears only briefly and is not named. She was referred to as a hero from above.

CHAPTER 5 –

Who are Modern Female Prayer Warriors?

We interviewed both men and women to find out their individual opinions about modern day female prayer warriors.

Narcia comments – "…A woman without fear, confident, covered by the armor of God. Ephesian 6:10

She thinks that a female prayer warrior identifies herself with her fellow man. Female warriors are in constant prayer. She is always ready with a sword, and she is guided by the Holy Spirit. She gets her strength from God."

Petra – "…thinks that a prayer warrior is an evangelist that fights against demons and satan. Her weapons are very powerful, and her strength comes from God."

Mary – "…is a spiritual warrior, prays 24-hours a day, is confident that she is maintaining a close relationship with God through the Holy Spirit, and she uses that connection with the Divine to fight the evil."

Lebrada – "…believes that a female warrior fights against the evil. When she falls she gets up. She is focused on fulfilling her objective."

Espenosa – "…she believes that a female prayer warrior is prepared with Wisdom. She takes time to study and to know the Word. She protects everything that has to do with God.

Lucia – "…a female prayer warrior fasts for the Word, she is very loving, she is faithful to God. She covers herself with God's shield. She recognizes spiritual warfare. She knows who she is."

Dr. Hudson – He believes, " a female prayer warrior is someone who goes to fight a battle or war, is strong and courageous, shows bravery, and a strategic approach."

Deacon - He believes that a female warrior is a person, that despite multiple problems and tribulations continues with her faith in God, recognizes the sacrifices of Yeshua. She doesn't complain."

David – He believes that a female prayer warrior is a soldier of Yeshua, full of love for God, does what pleases the Lord. The sword of the Holy Spirit crushes satan in two."

Lorena – She believes that the female prayer warrior struggles every day and has faith in God, loves God, fights for God, and appreciates God."

The central idea of a female prayer warrior is to fight evil.

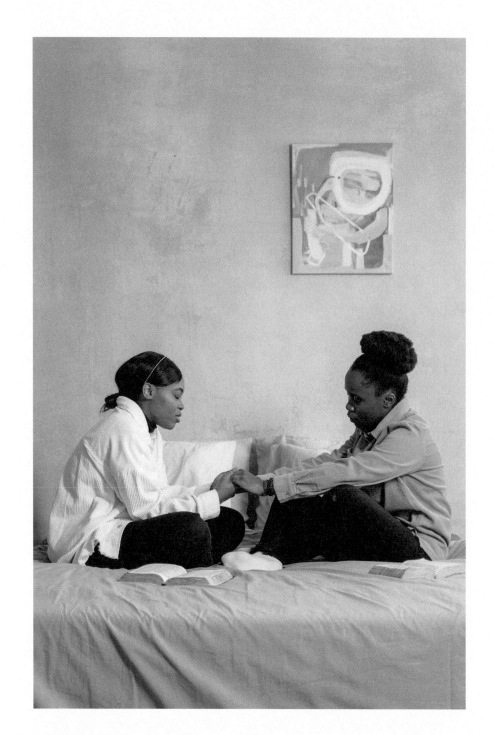

CHAPTER 6 –

Confession of a Female Prayer Warrior

Happy moments of my life –

- Finding God

- Adoring God

- Spending time with Him

- Participating in the PACE program, a non-profit organization to keep Senior Citizens independent and aging in place at home.

PACE stands for program of all inclusive care for the elderly. I joined PACE after being referred to this agency for lack of appropriate medical insurance. I was impressed with the warmth and love from all the staff. I suffered an unexpected stroke and due to PACE's efficiency, I was taken to the hospital in less than one hour only to be saved from being crippled. They have taken care of all my medical problems, appointments, and therapies in the clinic and in my home. If I needed something like a microwave, they provided it. They have delivered meals, laundered my clothing, and set up a woman to bathe me. All my medication is provided.

Their life enrichment program is highly effective in keeping the mind active. The PT department has been key to my spinal cord rehabilitation. When I was exhausted, they sent me to a place for a respite. PACE provided a bed overnight. They arrange my eye, dental, hearing, and multiple other medical appointments.

A special thanks to my PACE Social Worker, Tiffany Presberry.

- Knowing that my mother is going to Heaven and that I will see her again one day

- Having my sister friend, Maureen, in my life.

- The creation of a Non-Profit foundation to feed the children of the Philippines

- Spreading the Word of God by authoring books and using social media

- Recruiting souls for God

- Showing other people in wheelchairs that it is not the end of the world if you put God in your life

- Supporting my compassionate Paster Ryan and his family

- My adventures as a Forensic Pathologist

- Traveling all over the world

- Any smile of a child

- And more…

This list is about the Sad moments of my life –

- The death of my Mother
- The continual sexual abuse of my biological father
- Offending God with my sins
- To be in a wheelchair from a spinal injury

As you see, there are more happy moments than sad by living life for God as I have.

CHAPTER 7 –

Testimonials of Prayer Warriors

Elena's Experiences-

I have multiple examples of interactions by satanic forces of evil however, for the purpose of this book, only the following are included -

1. When I moved into this house, the previous owner was in a wheelchair and died in this house. It was vacant for 7 years. When I moved in, there was demonic activity. There were footsteps in the upstairs area. I contacted my pastor who came to get rid of them. The attempt they made to choke me to death didn't work. I called out the name of Yeshua barely able to get this out of my mouth from the strangulating choke hold. This attack took place on three occasions which I was able to cast evil out simply by using the authoritative name of Yeshua. I learned that even if all you can do is mumble his name, you can cast out any demon. The demons fly out immediately. If I used the name, Jesus, they leave after a while. This demonstrated to me the powerful name of Yeshua.

2. I was in my bedroom and was attacked by Beelzebub, the prince of demons. The name appears in the Bible in Mark 3:22, Matthew 12:24-27, Matthew 10:25, and Luke 11:15. He was pulling my hand and I could see the fire of hell behind

him. There were thousands of legions of demons behind him. I tried to cast him out but failed, but then I called out the name of Jesus who came to me dressed in white and pulled me away from the handhold of a powerful demon. Ephesians 6:12 says, "…for we wrestle not against flesh and blood, but against principalities, against powers, against the rulers of the darkness of this world…"

In every case, God won the battle, and I was able to rid my house of demons.

3. I had a car accident. In the medical workup, they found a tumor in the left adrenal gland, which looked benign. The right kidney from a CT scan and MRI showed a definite cancer mass. After surgery, no cancer was found to the surprise and astonishment of the surgeon. But I was always confident that God was my Savior and was always with me, and he was.

4. To be alive – I have had multiple near-death experiences – I was in a diabetic coma for two weeks where I could hear people around me talking and the doctors discussing my case.

5. Another time, a small car I was in stopped at an intersection and a truck was about to T-bone the car, but the driver of the truck was able to stop just in time.

6. I had another near-death experience during a spinal cord procedure that I could have died from, however, but I survived.

7. There were more than ten miracles, one after another.
   - I became homeless and needed to travel to Kentucky to be incarcerated. A "friend" offered to drive me to the Greyhound bus station. Once we arrived at the station as I got out of his car, I could only carry one of my two pieces of luggage. Thinking he would get out of the car and help get the other piece out for me, instead, he drove away. I was robbed of my luggage. The miracles began to unfold. The bag I had contained my personal ID and

$5.00 I had. I was standing outside the Greyhound station and went in to get onto the bus but the ticket that had been purchased by my real friend for me hadn't given me the copy of the ticket. He assumed that by giving my name it would show up in the system as having purchased that ticket. That was not how it played out. Instead, I had to purchase a ticket.

- The next miracle was that the ticket sales person ended up buying my ticket.
- The next miracle had to do with my health. I had a diabetic episode on the bus. I asked God to guide me, and he told me to go to a restaurant and get a packet of sugar and mix it with water which I did. When I got to Kentucky, I was given a Krispy Kreme donut by the owner of the Bakery. After that, I needed some place to stay overnight until I could call my friends the next day to ask them for money. I turned around and saw a chain store that was open 24 hours. I went in and had another diabetic episode.
- That led to the next miracle, that one of the employees was kind enough to call for an ambulance. The EMS ambulance took me to a Catholic hospital where they stabilized my diabetes.
- Subsequently, the next miracle involved the Chaplin on call who sent me to the Hotel that belonged to the hospital.
- It was at that hotel that there was only one room available. They agreed that I could stay there with only my word that I would be able to pay them the next day. I only had a penny in my wallet at the time.
- The following day another miracle was about to happen. The receptionist took me to a grocery store to call my friends for money to pay the hotel bill. They wired the exact amount I needed to pay the hotel bill off.

As you can see, God took care of my every need in His time.

Stephanie's Experiences-

Some of the darkest moments in my life had to do with academic challenges, health trauma, and failed relationships.

The feeling of inadequacy as a child impacted my self-image but it never rattled my faith in Jesus. I was born with an eye deficit that impacted my ability to read fluently thus lacking reading comprehension. The effort I put out was as much as my eyes could handle for any given assignment. I didn't know that after reading a paragraph, I didn't have a clue what I had read. The only way I found that out was when I took the test and the material looked new. I didn't recall having read most of the history questions. Story problems in math were confusing and even more so once they added alphabetical letters to the equation.

When I finished my college degree in three ½ years by taking summer classes each academic year, I was so happy to travel to two states away from my home to learn my art of therapy in clinical settings. The requirement to complete the internship was 3 months each placement.

At the end of the second placement, a month before my Board Exam and getting married in my home state, I found out I have cancer. I only had 3 weeks to go, and the doctor said I absolutely could not finish the placement instead, I had to be hospitalized. My parents and family were in my home state hours away by car. The biopsy, lymphangiogram, and treatment all started without them, and I was only 22 years old. The radiation made my throat feel like it was on fire and swallowing was extremely uncomfortable. Everything tasted like salt, and I never got used to drinking saltwater or eating a teaspoon of salt. Thus, I lost 35 lbs. in 5 weeks during the month of radiation. My hair fell out just in time for my wedding, which we had to postpone a month having to change all arrangements from out of state. My family had to help with that. My dress was made at the last minute due to my new emaciated body.

This marriage "made in heaven," ended up in a divorce that I never saw coming. We were Christians and I never even knew a divorced couple let alone become a divorcee myself. The break-up was heart rendering since I never saw it coming and the grounds for the divorce were not what really happened. The marriage was annulled. I prayed for children for 14 years only to find out he didn't want children. I'm sure we discussed children before and throughout the marriage.

JESUS ANSWERS PRAYERS

The throat burning was the first time I ever cried out to the Lord for help. The miracle of an immediate cold ensued to soothe my throat that first day of radiation. I knew that God cared about me and was with me. I was part of a Charismatic community and was prayed over more than once by the members multiple times. I was cancer free by the end of the month of radiation and am 40+ years past that without a recurrence. I am a cancer survivor that was touched by the healing power of God, through the Holy Spirit.

I remember as a 7-year-old being on my knees praying to Jesus to heal my eye. I remember energetically bouncing up and running to the mirror to look, study, and exercise the eye that had never looked to the left of midline.

I remember as a first grader in a Catholic grade school, attending a movie in the College auditorium. The movie was called "The Miracle of San Juan Capistrano" . It was about an infant whose parents were dead and he was left on the steps of a monastery. They raised him and he almost died of a scorpion's sting. After he recovered, one day he ventured to a forbidden room he had never been in. It was a room filled with greater than life-sized statues of saints and a Crucifix with Jesus hanging from it. The boy slowly walked through to the far end of the large room where the Jesus was. Suddenly, Jesus was alive and came down off the Cross and sat in a red velvet royal chair. The boy sat on Jesus' lap and Jesus asked him," What would you like, my son?" The boy replied, "To be with my parents." Jesus answered him, "You will be with them in Paradise today." And just then the Monks came rushing up the stairs and through the open door only to see a bright light that made them fall to their knees and stair up to the magnificent image of the boy curled up in the chair and the chair was ascending into the light ray coming in through the window. He was on his way to Heaven to be with his parents. I remember tears streaming down my face and I felt out of my body elevating up with them… when the film ended, the lights of the auditorium came on and my classmates began to leave the room row-by-row. I couldn't move, I was still caught up in the supernatural moment. This experience changed my life.

The next amazing moment was listening to Father Walters read from scripture about Jesus moving through the crowd and laying hands on people in the crowd who he healed, the blind man, the lady who was bleeding, the person with leprosy, the girl he raised from the dead… I remember saying to Jesus that I wanted to be just like him when I grow up.

Some years after the divorce, I met my wonderful husband. And after 18 years of praying for a child, I had my one pregnancy at 40 and had a baby. She has been my miracle and I treasure her life as the answer to my prayer. God's timing is perfect.

When I was 46 years old, my left eye was healed, and I can now move it to the left. The result of this personal answer to prayer after 30+ years was even greater than just being able to move my eye. The correction impacted my potential as a student. I would never have gone back to graduate school to get a Master of Science degree if Jesus hadn't provided the missing movement that gave me reading comprehension. I had confidence for the first time that I could conquer the mountain of reading that this step would require, and I was successful.

Today, my lifelong prayer of healing has been fulfilled. I was introduced to a manual therapy technique that requires the laying on of hands with a gentle touch that helps the body heal. There is no doubt in my mind where the healing comes from. Each day I have the opportunity to watch Miracles happen with my patients. I am truly blessed with this gift. Everything in God's time.

CHAPTER 8 –

Where We Came From

Ephesians 1:3 "Blessed be the God and Father of our Lord Jesus Christ, who has blessed us in Christ with every spiritual blessing in the heavenly places, even as he chose us in him before the foundation of the world, that we should be holy and blameless before him."

Simply put God, the Creator or the universe and all living things seen and unseen, created us. God knew us before we were born implying a spiritual origin implanted by the Holy Spirit at conception.

All are created by God, our Heavenly Father from whom all good things come.

If we are of God's own making then we come forth as a member of the family of God. We have been blessed with being gifted with a physical human body that can procreate with God and a soul that is our spiritual nature. Angels have no gender, nor do they have souls, yet are gifted and purposeful in God's creation of Heaven and Earth. They play a huge part in all of God's Kingdom and in the history of humanity.

God created us to *know, love, and serve. We are made in His image and likeness. He became one of us to save us from the sin that entered the world by way of a jealous spiritual being, satan.* (I refuse to honor that creature by capitalizing the name and those beings and his followers due to his disobedience, arrogance, and evil nature having given up his position. He could have and should have made better choices when he had the opportunity. Or this was the plan all along. He does not have the ability to *create, only duplicates.* He cannot read our thoughts. He is shattered by our prayers given to use by Yeshua and our Blessed Mother Mary, the Mother of God, the human/divine Jesus Christ. Thus, women Prayer Warriors have our marching orders as our call here on earth.

We are here on this planet because we are in the Book of Life in Heaven, or we better make sure we are for this has everlasting consequences.

We have the gift of FAITH and we have put on the armor of God.

BE NOT AFRAID says our Shephard.

CHAPTER 9 –

Why We Are Here

Ephesians 1:15-23

We women warriors are here to bring forth God's plan for humanity in our days and time allotted us on earth to serve our Creator, Counselor, King, Father, our Savior, the Almighty God of Israel and to follow the guidance of the Holy Spirit that brings forth the souls of His offspring.

We bring God into our daily lives each minute spending quiet time with him daily. Prayer is our communion with God. He blesses his faithful with gifts of the Holy Spirit and virtues. We pray and ask to be open to these gifts that are ours from Heaven and freely given. It delights Yeshua to spend time in his Heavenly portal showering us with his golden light of grace and Divine presence filling us with his unconditional love.

We are bathed in his Holy Oil from Heaven that will kindle the fire of God's Glory. Our purpose here on Earth is to procreate and lead others toward God, His Light, and His eternal Life in Heaven with all the Saints and Angels to adore and worship Him without a care and unceasingly.

Everyone is called to be a Saint, a follower, the sheep of His flock. We are here for His purpose. Truly, He doesn't worry about our politics, finances, or popularity.

In prayer one day, I heard the whisper of Jesus giving me the vision and calling to declare and dispense the Angels of Mercy down from Heaven to usher in the day of the Lord. He will arrive bringing fire upon the Earth, knocking on each person's door one last time to give a chance to repent, to listen to his voice, to love and be loved by the Savior and Shepard of His flock who are lost. He is gathering in the Harvest spoken about in the Bible, God's story of all age's past, present, and to come.

We are the women warriors wearing the Armor of God that He placed on us.

I wear the Armor knowing of this ultimate protection that was placed on me by our Divine LOVER.

Our Shephard, the Lord, our savior, the Son of God, our Lover, our brother, a fellow human resurrected Lord of Lords, encourages us to BE NOT AFRAID, throughout the Word of God's Holy Bible.

Put on the armor of God to fight in this battle written in the Book of Life that we each are to finish here and now, that is ushering in the New Jerusalem, the Heaven on Earth, the closing chapter of time and the physical world. The call is simple, do as He says to you. Listen to Jesus and spend time praising, singing, being thankful, grateful, joyful, sharing in the Grace from Heaven, just for you! All of this would have happened if you were the only person created by God. You are precious in His sight. He loves you and died for you to free you from sin that entered the world because of a disobedient angel who refused to serve God. God is blessing us with every living thing around us, the air we breathe, the grass, the birds and animals, the water, the wind, the sky, the planets in the heavens above. All were placed here for you to enjoy.

Rise above the physical world opening your mind, soul, and heart to Jesus asking for a sincere relationship with Him, instead of what man offers you in worldly comforts, prizes, and empty promises. None of it will last and you surely cannot take it with you when you leave.

Trust in God and He will act.

Obey His commandments and follow the Golden Rule

> Matthew 7:12 "Do unto others as you would have them do to you, for this sums up the Law and the Prophets."

> Matthew 7:1-5 "Do not judge, or you too will be judged. …For in the same way you judge others, you will be judged, and with the measure you give will be the measure you get.

> Luke 10: 27-28 "And he answered, You shall love the Lord your God and with all your heart, with all your soul, and with all your strength, and with all your whole mind, and your neighbor as yourself…do this and you shall live."

Ten Commandments

1. Thou shalt have no other Gods before me.
2. Thou shalt not make unto thee any graven images
3. Thou shalt not take the name of the Lord thy God in vain.
4. Remember the Sabbath day to keep it holy.
5. Honor they father and thy mother.
6. Thou shalt not kill.
7. Thou shalt not commit adultery.
8. Thou shalt not steal.
9. Thou shalt not bear false witness against thy neighbor
10. Thou shalt not covet anything that is thy neighbor's

CHAPTER 10 –

Where We Are Headed

Ephesians 2:4-10

We are headed into the New Jerusalem, Heaven, to the place prepared for us. If we have fulfilled our purpose while here, we will be raised up, maybe because of the times without having to experience death. We will be raised up one way or another, to our Mansion that will be the Banquet Table of the Lord. We prepare our own Banquet table by the good that we do during our time on Earth serving God and our neighbors. There will be no crying, nor pain, nor death anymore!!! Alleluia!!!

We will see the face of God and live. We will see the streets of gold we have never seen. We fill be filled with God's LOVE we have never known on earth. Colors in Heaven are indescribable according to those who died, saw the Heavenly places, and returned to tell us all about their real encounters with the Holy of Holy, the Angels, and those who passed before us.

The day of judgment is coming upon the earth as I type this warning.

Be prepared.

Repent.

Open your heart.

Love the Lord with your whole heart, your whole soul, and with your mind.

BE NOT AFRAID says our Shephard.

> This is all God asks of us and to accept His Son, Yeshua's gift of salvation.

> …And to spend time with Him remembering He is your strength and eternal LIGHT to the nations.

Our Father, who art in Heaven, hallowed be thy name.

Thy Kingdom come, thy Will be done, on earth as it is in Heaven.

Give us this day, our daily bread.

And forgive us our trespasses, as we forgive those who trespass against us.

And lead us not into temptation but deliver us from evil. For thine is the Kingdom, and the Power, and the Glory, forever.

Amen

> Be God's light living through you in the ever-darkening world we live in.

> See you in Heaven and I pray your mansion is next to mine!!!

Don't worry…be HAPPY!!! There is nothing to fear in this world that God has not already conquered.

Be in communion with the Lord always bring Him into your day in all circumstances letting go of your fear of the future and planning.

Let him be part of your life moment by moment.

Ephesians 6:10 - "Be strong in the Lord and in his mighty power." Wear your armor – the shield of Faith, the sword of the Spirit his Word, loins of Truth, the helmet of Salvation, the shoes of the preparation of the Gospel of Peace, the breastplate of Righteousness.

ASK Him … listen… do His Will and what He says.

Be Prayerful, be Truthful, and be His Warrior. Most of all LOVE.

Printed in the United States
by Baker & Taylor Publisher Services